SO YOU CALL YOURSELF A CHICAGO CUBS FAN?

DAVID FURGESS

SPP-001

Shibe Park Publishing
PO Box 522
Milford, CT 06460
USA

shibeparkpublishing@blogspot.com

INTRODUCTION

So how does a 7 year old kid from Bridgeport, Connecticut become a Chicago Cubs fan? It happened in July of 1968 following a New York Yankees-California Angels game at the original Yankee Stadium. I was with my grandfather in a souvenir store called Manny's Baseball Land, when I noticed a Chicago Cubs pennant for sale. I asked my grandfather to buy it for me and that's how I became a Cubs fan right there. Nobody in my family of New York Yankees fans could understand it. I really couldn't explain it myself, I just wanted to be different.

I really didn't know anything about Cubs history at that point (since I was only 7 years old.) But I began to read about the Cubs. My main sources were a library book called *My Greatest Day In Baseball* (which had stories by Three Finger Brown and Frank Chance.) There was also a World Series baseball card set put out by Fleer in 1970 that had detailed stories about every World Series. I was surprised to learn the Cubs were quite successful in the early part of the 1900's (appearing in 10 World Series from 1906-1945.) I also read *Baseball Digest* whenever I could.

To be honest it wasn't easy being a Cub fan in Connecticut in the late 60's and early 70's. Almost every kid in my school was a New York Mets fan and I got their abuse on a daily basis. The Cubs collapse of 1969 found me expelled from school for 2 days for punching out an obnoxious Met fan at school (I actually gave the kid a black eye which I felt quite proud of.) Then there were the times I attended Met-Cubs games at Shea Stadium in the 69-73 period. I always wore my Cubs hat and I got abuse from every corner of Shea. At the time I think I was the only Cub fan in the stadium or on the whole east coast of the USA for that matter.

In many ways being a Cub fan in Connecticut was much tougher than being one in Chicago. I was in the heart of enemy country. While the Cubs and Mets are no longer rivals (due to Bub Seling's bumbling) back in the 70's they were hated rivals. I really didn't feel a rivalry with the Cardinals in Connecticut. However, once I got Direct TV in 2000 and was able to see Cub games on a daily basis I began to cultivate a deep dislike of the Cardinals (thanks in large part to their obnoxious TV man Al Hrbosky.

I have seen a lot of ups and downs in my 44 years of being a Cub fan (mostly downs.) But I must I had never heard that stupid "billy goat" story until just a few years ago (I think that whole thing was cooked up by the media.) If the 1945 curse was true then what prevented the Cubs winning a World Series from 1908-1944? I think the whole thing is a lot of nonsense.

Here in 2013 it's still not easy being a Cub fan but not for the reasons you might think. In recent years I have had to endure Chip Carey, those hideous yuppie rooftop clubs that have made Wrigley Field look like a pinball machine and the fair weather Cub fans who show up when the team is winning with their "let's go Cubbies" chants then disappear when they are losing (for the record I have never called the Cubs the Cubbies in my life!) Then there is the awful 7th inning stretch singing torture (but enough of my ranting!)

This book was put together over a weekend an is intended to separate the true Cub fan from the pretenders that have sprouted up in recent years. The questions trace every era of Cub history so dig in and see what kind of Cub fan you are. So you call yourself a Chicago Cubs fan?

David Furgess-Salem, CT (11-15-13.)

SO YOU CALL YOURSELF A CHICAGO CUBS FAN?

200 QUESTIONS THAT FORM THE ULTIMATE CUB TRIVIA CHALLENGE

DEDICATED TO:

Ted Savage, Roe Skidmore, the College Of Coaches, Ray Blades, Jim Qualls, Moe Thacker, Andre Dawson, Glen Hobbie, Cuno Barrigan, Jack Brickhouse, Bert Furgess Sr., Adolpho Phillips, Dick Calmus, Dave Gumpert, Randy Bobb and Jim Cosman. Special thanks to Skippy The Cat!

Question #1

This former New York Giants All Star first baseman replaced Leo Durocher as Cubs manager during the 1972 season. Who was he?

Question #2

This 1970 Cub got a hit in his only MLB at bat and got a hit and ended his career with a batting average of 1.000. He was traded to the Chicago White Sox after the 1970 season and never reached the big leagues again. Can You name him?

Question #3

This Cub pitcher was traded to the Milwaukee Brewers for outfielder Jose Cardenal. He would later win 20 in a season for the Brewers and was an American League All Star. Can you name him?

Question #4

This two time Cleveland Indians' All Star first baseman was traded by the Cubs to the Montreal Expos for pitcher Steve Renko and outfielder Larry Biitner. Who is he?

Question #5

The Cubs received pitchers Bob Scanlan and Chuck McElroy from the Philadelphia Phillies for what former Cub All Star reliever?

Question #6

The Cubs purchased the contract of this three time All Star outfielder in 1981. Can you name him?

Question #7

The Cubs received pitchers Darold Knowles, Bob Locker and infielder Manny Trillo from the Oakland A's in a trade for what Cub outfielder?

Question #8

The Cubs received pitchers Bill Johnson and Dick Ruthven from the Philadelphia Phillies for the future American League Cy Young Award winner and AL MVP. Who is he?

Question #9

This former Pittsburgh Pirate slugger hit 50 homers for the Cubs over two seasons in the 1950's. Can you name him?

Question #10

What Cub relief pitcher was nicknamed "The Vulture"?

Question #11

Name the Cub outfielder who broke up the perfect game bid by New York Met pitcher Tom Seaver in the 9th inning of game in 1969?

Question #12

Name the Cub infield prospect who was the key component in the 2003 trade with the Pittsburgh Pirates that brought Aramis Ramirez and Ken Lofton to the Cubs?

Question #13

Name the former first round draft pick of the Cubs and 1988 Olympian who was one the biggest disappointments in Cub amateur draft history?

Question #14

In 1966 The Cubs traded pitchers Bob Buhl and Larry Jackson to the Philadelphia Phillies for what future Cub pitching great?

Question #15

Name the Cub whose hit knocked in Pete Rose in his famous collision with Ray Fosse in the 1970 MLB All Star game?

Question #16

The Cubs received pitcher Dave Crouthers and infielders Jerry Hairston and Mike Fontenot in a trade with the Baltimore Orioles for what Cubs player?

Question #17

The Cubs received All Star pitcher Dave LaRoche from this Minnesota Twins in a trade for this former Cub 20 game winning pitcher. Can you name him?

Question #18

Who was the Cub pitcher who homered in game seven of the 2003 NLCS?

Question #19

Name the Cub All Star pitcher who was bombed by the San Francisco Giants in game one of the 1989 NLCS?

Question #20

The Cubs received future All Star catcher Randy Hundley and future 20 game winning pitcher Bill Hands in a trade with what National League team?

Question #21

This Cub great was the 1961 Rookie Of The Year. Can you name him?

Question #22

This former New York Yankees shortstop and front office executive managed the Cubs in the 1980's. Can you name him?

Question #23

Name the first black player to be signed by the Cubs in team history?

Question #24

This former Cub became the first black manager in organized baseball. Can you name him?

Question #25

The Cubs had a chance to acquire Hall Of Fame outfielder Frank Robinson in the early 70's but the deal was killed when the Cubs refused to part with this outfield prospect. Who is he?

Question #26

This former Cub first baseman was the son of Hollywood Squares TV game show host Peter Marshall. Can you name him?

Question #27

This former Cub outfielder and National League Rookie Of The Year had a 30 game hitting streak during his rookie season with the Cubs. Who is he?

Question #28

What Cub pitcher was the first black pitcher to fire a no-hitter in MLB history. Can you name him?

Question #29

This former Cub Rookie Of The Year infielder tragically died in a plane crash prior to the 1964 season. Can you name him?

Question #30

What famous baseball executive planted the famous ivy at outfield wall at Wrigley Field?

Question #31

This Cub pitcher would become a National League All Star as a member of the Montreal Expos. He was later the General Manager of the 2002 World Champion Los Angeles Angels. Can you name him?

Question #32

Actor Chuck Connors was a member of the 1950 Cubs. What was the name of the TV show that brought him massive success in Hollywood?

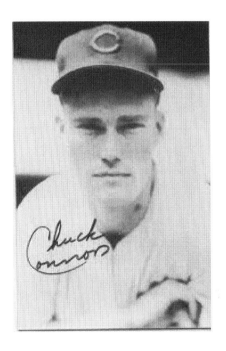

Question #33

The Cubs acquired this future Hall Of Fame pitcher from the Boston Red Sox for first baseman Bill Buckner. Can you name him?

Question #34

The Cubs acquired minor leaguers Brian Guinn, Dave Wilder and Mark Leonette in a trade with the Oakland A's for what future Hall Of Fame pitcher?

Question #35

The Cubs traded All Star third baseman and four time National League batting champion Bill Madlock to the San Francisco Giants for this former New York Yankees All Star. Can you name him?

Question #36

The Cubs acquired Charlie Gilbert and Johnny Hudson from the Brooklyn Dodgers for what future Cub Hall Of Fame infielder?

Question #37

The Cubs acquired pitchers Al Nipper and Calvin Schiraldi in a trade with the Boston Red Sox for this Cub All Star pitcher. Who is he?

Question #38

What Cub manager was nicknamed "The Fordham Flash" during his playing days?

Question #39

This Hall Of Fame manager is best known as a New York Yankee. But prior to managing the Yankees he guided the Cubs to the World Series. Can you name him?

Question #40

This Hall Of Fame manager replaced Bob Kennedy and Lou Klein as the Cub skipper in the mid 60's. Can you name him?

Question #41

Name the Cub pitcher who threw a no-hitter against the San Diego Padres in 1972?

Question #42

Name the ballpark where Cub pitcher Carlos Zambrano tossed his 2008 no-hitter against the Houston Astros?

Question #43

Name the Cub pitcher who threw a no-hitter against the St. Louis Cardinals in 1960?

Question #44

Name the Cub player and future Milwaukee Brewers manager who was the final victim in Los Angeles Dodgers' Sandy Koufax's perfect game against the Cubs in 1965?

Question #45

This former Cub pitcher has the most wins by a Jewish pitcher in MLB history. Can you name him?

Question #46

The Cubs traded this All Star left-handed pitcher to the Oakland A's for outfielder Rick Monday. Can you name him?

Question #47

Name the only Cub to win back to back National League MVP awards?

Question #48

This Cub Hall Of Fame slugger stills holds the MLB record for most RBI's in a single season with 191. Can you name him?

Question #49

What Cub All Star shortstop was later a player-manager for the Chicago White Sox?

Question #50

Name the future Hall Of Fame outfielder who the Cubs traded to the St. Louis Cardinals in 1964 for a package of players that included pitcher Ernie Broglio?

Question #51

Name the Cub outfielder who won the National Rookie Of The Year award and the National League MVP for the Cubs?

Question #52

The Cubs signed this free agent pitcher from the Houston Astros in 1991. He never won a game for the Cubs in two disappointing seasons. Can you name him?

Question #53

Ernie Banks was one of two players in Cub history with the last name Banks. Can you name the other one?

Question #54

Carlos Zambrano was one of two players in Cub history with the last name Zambrano. Can you name the other one?

Question #55

This future All Star knuckleball pitcher was traded by the Cubs to the San Diego Padres for pitcher Dick Selma in 1969. Can you name him?

Question #56

This former Cub first round draft pick was the last player in major league history to win a World Series deciding game with a so-called "walk-off home run." Can you name him?

Question #57

The Cubs traded this former American League MVP to the Chicago White Sox for Sammy Sosa & Ken Patterson. Can you name him?

Question #58

Cub pitching great Greg Maddux won his 300th career game back with the Cubs. What team did he defeat for win #300?

(Greg Maddux wins his 300th game)

Question #59

This Atlanta Braves pitcher gave up Ernie Banks' 500th career home run. Can you name him?

Question #60

The Cubs traded former first round draft pick and future All Star Joe Carter to the Cleveland Indians for this future Cub Cy Young Award winner. Can you name him?

Question #61

What team did the Cubs defeat for their first post season series win since 1908?

Question #62

The Cubs drafted this player in the 2006 MLB Rule 5 Draft and sold him to the Cincinnati Reds. He would later become an American League All Star & American League MVP. Who is he?

Question #63

This former New York Giants NFL Pro Bowl defensive back once played for the Cubs Appalachian League team in Huntington, West Virginia. Can you name him?

Question #64

The Cubs drafted this player with the number 1 overall pick in the 1982 MLB amateur draft (ahead of Dwight Gooden.) Can you name him?

Question #65

The Cubs selected this future All Star outfielder with the number 2 pick in the 1981 MLB amateur draft. Can you name him?

Question #66

This former Cub first round draft pick would later make it to the majors as a combination pitcher/outfielder specialty player for the Milwaukee Brewers. Can you name him?

Question #67

This Cub right-hander pitched a gutty game to win the one game playoff tie-breaker game between the Cubs and Giants in 1998. Can you name him?

Question #68

This former Pittsburgh Pirates outfielder was the key figure in one of the most controversial plays in Cub history during the 2003 NLCS. Can you name him?

Question #69

How many future Hall Of Fame players were on the 1969 Chicago Cubs?

Question #70

This home grown Cub was lost to Colorado in the 1992 expansion draft. He would later win World Series championships as a player and a manager. Who is he?

Question #71

What former Cub manager took over as the team's General Manager to replace Dallas Green?

Question #72

This former Cub #1 draft pick was the son of former MLB player Dave May. Can you name him?

Question #73

The Cubs traded this outfielder to the Pittsburgh Pirates for future Cub 20 game winning pitcher Jon Lieber. Can you name him?

Question #74

This former Cub first round draft pick was better known for intentionally striking an opposing player in the on deck circle in a college game than anything he did in pro baseball. Can you name this Cub first round bust?

Question #75

Can you name the Cub pitcher that was traded to the Los Angeles Dodgers for shortstop Cesar Izturis?

Question #76

This former Cub first base prospect was traded to the Florida Marlins for future Cub All Star first baseman Derek Lee. Can you name him?

Question #77

This former Cub first round pick was considered a major disappointment and was shipped to the Baltimore Orioles. He later came back to haunt the Cubs by winning a World Series ring with the hated St. Louis Cardinals. Can you name him?

Question #78

This former Cub holds the MLB record for the highest batting average ever in a World Series in 1990 (.750) Can you name him?

Question #79

Can you name the Cubs home ballpark prior to Wrigley Field?

Question #80

What was the name of Wrigley Field when it was first built in 1914?

David Furgess

Question #81

What was the name of Wrigley Field from the years 1920-1925?

Question #82

How many World Series have the Chicago Cubs won while playing at Wrigley Field?

Question #83

What was the Cubs home ballpark when they last won the World Series?

Question #84

What year was the name Wrigley Field first used in association with the Cubs' home ballpark?

Question #85

What was the first World Series to be held at Wrigley Field?

Question #86

Name the Cubs' home ballpark that was located at Polk and Lincoln Streets in Chicago?

Question #87

At one time the Cubs owned two separate ballparks named Wrigley Field. The first one was obviously located in Chicago. Where was the other Wrigley Field located?

Question #88

Can you name the American League team that played their home games at the "other" Wrigley Field?

Question #89

This Cub pitcher of the early 70's was once traded by the Cincinnati Reds for Hall Of Fame outfielder Frank Robinson. Can you name him?

Question #90

The Cubs traded this four time All Star infielder to the San Diego Padres for outfielder Jerry Morales. Can you name him?

Question #91

The Cubs received catcher George Mitterwald in a trade with the Minnesota Twins for this former Cub All Star catcher. Who is he?

Question #92

What was the Cubs original nickname? (which they first used during the 1876 season)

Question #93

This one time Cub catcher was the base runner for the New York Mets in the famous "shoe polish" play at first base in the 1969 World Series. Can you name him?

Question #94

This one time Cub pitcher was the losing pitcher in the famous game 6 of the 1986 World Series for the Boston Red Sox. Can you name him?

Question #95

This Cub All Star pitcher was acquired from the Philadelphia Phillies in a 1939 trade for Kirby Higbe, Ray Harrell and Joe Marty. Can you name him?

Question #96

This Cleveland Indians Hall Of Fame infielder was both a manager and broadcaster for the Cubs. Can you name him?

Question #97

This two time Cub All Star was drafted from the St. Louis Cardinals in the 1980 MLB Rule 5 draft. Can you name him?

Question #98

This young Cub outfielder earned a place in manager Leo Durocher's doghouse with his erratic outfield play in 1969. Can you name him?

Question #99

What was the Cubs nickname just prior to taking the name Chicago Cubs for the 1903 season?

Question #100

Name the Cub manager who made an appearance in the 1960's TV show The Munsters?

Question #101

This Cuban free agent signed the largest bonus in Cub team history. Who is he?

Question #102

Name the Cub Hall Of Fame first baseman and manager who later managed the New York Yankees for two seasons in the 1920's?

Question #103

What team is tied with the 1906 Cubs in having the most wins in a single season with 116?

1906 Chicago Cubs
NL Champions

Question #104

This Cub All Star infielder and four time National League Batting champion was a starter on the 1979 World Champion Pittsburgh Pirates. Can you name him?

Question #105

Can you name the Cub Hall Of Fame outfielder who played 1117 consecutive games?

Question #106

Name the Cub outfield speedster who was traded to the Oakland A's for pitcher Bob Locker in 1972?

Question #107

This former Cub third baseman was an accomplished trumpet player and was married to Grammy Award winning singer Sue Raney. Can you name him?

Question #108

This former Cub pitcher tragically took his own life following his poor performances for the California Angels in the 1986 ALCS. Can you name him?

Question #109

This one time Cub slugger led the National League in home runs in 1979 and 1982. Can you name him?

Question #110

This Cub great was the only Chicago Cub to win the National League Rookie Of The Year award and a National League Batting title. Can you name him?

Question #111

This Cub fan favorite was nicknamed "The Sarge." Can you name him?

Question #112

This former Cub All Star first baseman was the last Cub to win a National League Batting title. Can you name him?

Question #113

This former Cub first round draft pick (#3 overall) was a major bust but finally played with the Cubs in a limited role in 2011. Can you name him?

Question #114

What player received the largest bonus by the Cubs for a player taken in the amateur draft?

Question #115

What player received the largest bonus by the Cubs for a foreign signing?

Question #116

This outfielder was taken with the 6th overall pick in the first round of the 2003 MLB amateur draft and was a complete bust. He would later try to make it as a pitcher with the Boston Red Sox. Can you name him?

Question #117

The Cubs have had only one #1 overall pick in the MLB amateur draft's history. Can you name him?

Question #118

This former Cub first round draft pick ended his MLB career with 569 home runs, 1835 RBI's and over 3,000 hits (but only played in 258 games as a Cub.) Who is he?

Question #119

This former Cub first round draft pick (#3 overall) made the news for wearing a t-shirt that said "I was Frey-ed and Zimmer-ed in Chicago" when he was traded to the Texas Rangers. Who is he?

Question #120

Can you name the former Cub first round draft pick (#3 overall) who was traded to the Cleveland Indians for pitcher Rick Sutcliffe in 1984?

Question #121

The Cubs drafted this player #2 overall in the 1967 MLB amateur draft ahead of future All Stars Ted Simmons, Jon Matlack and Bobby Grich. Can you name him?

Question #122

The Cubs traded this former first round draft pick (#10 overall) to the Chicago White Sox for pitcher Matt Karchner in a 1998 trade deadline deal. Can you name him?

Question #123

This St. Louis Cardinals Hall Of Fame pitcher was (7-1 with a 1.81 ERA) with the 1938 National League champion Chicago Cubs. Can you name him?

Question #124

This lefthander led the 1918 National League champion Chicago Cubs with 22 wins and an ERA of 1.74, can you name him?

Question #125

This one time Cub pitching ace had the nickname "Big Daddy." Who is he?

Question #126

This Cub great won the National League MVP during the Cubs 1945 National League pennant winning season. Can you name him?

Question #127

This former Oakland A's first round draft pick signed as a free agent with the Cubs following Greg Maddux's departure to Atlanta as a free agent in 1992. Who is he?

Question #128

The Cubs traded pitchers Kyle Lohse and Jason Ryan to this Minnesota Twins for pitcher Scott Downs and this three time American League All Star closer? Can you name him?

Question #129

This two time National League Triple Crown winner hit .380 with 39 homers and 149 RBI's for the Cubs 1929 National League Champion team. Can you name him?

Question #130

What American League team have the Cubs faced the most times in World Series play?

Question #131

This Cub Hall Of Fame outfielder played for Cubs World Series teams in 1929, 1932 and 1935. Can you name home?

Question #132

This Cub pitching great led the National League with 26 wins in 1927. He also served Babe Ruth's alleged "called shot" in the 1932 World Series. Can you name him?

Question #133

This Cub All Star pitcher's nickname was "The Arkansas Hummingbird." Can you name him?

Question #134

This Hall Of Fame pitcher won 6 games as a "spot starter" for the 1932 Cub National League championship team. Can you name him?

Question #135

This former New York Giant made the base running blunder that led to the Cubs defeating the Giants for the 1908 National League pennant. He would later become a starting member of the Cubs' 1918 National League championship team. Can you name him?

Question #136

This Cub outfielder earned high praise for preventing two criminals from setting fire to the American flag at Dodger Stadium in Los Angeles. Who is he?

Question #137

What was the Cubs nickname from 1890 to 1897?

Question #138

Name the only MLB team to be defeated by the Cubs in the World Series?

Question #139

This former Cub All Star pitcher was traded to the New York Yankees for pitcher Doug Bird and cash. Who is he?

Question #140

Name the only Cub Hall Of Fame player to be traded for a future Cubs broadcaster?

Question #141

This Cub pitcher totally lost his ability to throw strikes (aka Steve Blass disease) after he was traded to the New York Yankees. Can you name him?

Question #142

Name the Cub manager who is best known for his post game tirade with the press in 1983?

Question #143

Name the one time Cub manager who had previously been the first manager in San Diego Padres history?

Question #144

Name the Cub brother pitching combination with the most wins in team history?

Question #145

Name the Cub infielder with the same name as the undisputed heavyweight boxing champion of the late 1980's?

Question #146

This Cub Hall Of Fame pitcher had the nickname "Three Finger." Can you name him?

David Furgess

Question #147

Who was the Cubs' opponent in the first night game in Wrigley Field history?

Question #148

Who was the Cubs' opponent in the first "official" night game in Wrigley Field history?

Question #149

This former Cub infielder won a World Series ring as manager of the Oakland A's. Can you name him?

Question #150

This former Cub outfielder is best known for his home run that was called "The Shot Heard Around The World." Can you name him?

Question #151

What was the name given to the Cubs revolving manager experiment that took place during the 1961 and 1962 seasons?

Question #152

Who owned the Cubs prior to the Wrigley family purchasing the team in 1921?

Question #153

Who was the Cubs' owner when they won their only two World Series championships in 1907 & 1908?

Question #154

Name the pitcher who served up Sammy Sosa's 500ᵗʰ career home run?

Question #155

What pitcher served up Sammy Sosa's 62nd home run during the 1998 season?

Question #156

What pitcher surrendered Sammy Sosa's franchise record 66th home run in 1998?

Question #157

Who was the former Cub first round draft pick that was briefly a Cub broadcaster in the early 2000's?

Question #158

How many Cub managers have won manager of the year?

Question #159

Who was the first Cub manager to win National League manager of the year?

Question #160

Who was the former Cub who led the Colorado Rockies to their only World Series appearance as manager?

Question #161

What former Cub player has the most wins as a manager in MLB history?

Question #162

This Cub pitching great was the team's last hurler to win the National League pitcher's triple crown. Who is he?

Question #163

The Cubs acquired this future Hall Of Fame pitcher from the Philadelphia Phillies in a trade for catcher Pickles Dillhoefer, pitcher Mike Prendergast and cash. Can you name him?

Question #164

Name the first Cub pitcher to win to the National League pitcher's Triple Crown?

Question #165

This former Cub won the American League Rookie Of The Year Award and two American League Batting titles. Who is he?

Question #166

Name the first Cub player to win the National League MVP award?

Question #167

Can you name the Philadelphia Phillies Hall Of Fame outfielder who played a key role for the Cubs on their 1935 National League championship team?

Question #168

Can you name the only Cub catcher to win the National League MVP award?

Question #169

This Cub slugger won the National League MVP in 1952. His nickname was "The Honker." Can you name him?

Question #170

The Cub pitcher won the first National League Cy Young Award in team history. Who is he?

Question #171

This Cub relief pitcher was the only Cubs' reliever to ever win a National League Cy Young award. Who is he?

Question #172

This Cub reliever set the team record for 53 saves in a season. Can you name him?

Question #173

This former Cub manager won the American League MVP as a player for the California Angels in the late 1970's. Can you name him?

Question #174

Who was the first Cub pitcher to win the National League Rookie Of The Year award?

Question #175

Name the only former National League Rookie Of The Year to later manage the Cubs?

Question #176

Who was the first black manager in Chicago Cubs history?

Question #177

Name the only Cub catcher to win the National League Rookie Of The Year award?

Question #178

The Cubs acquired pitchers Antonio Alfonseca and Matt Clement from the Florida Marlins for this future National League Rookie Of Year and All Star. Can you name him?

Question #179

Can you name the only Cub to win the MLB All Star game MVP award?

Question #180

This former Cub led all of major league baseball in the decade of the 1990's in hits (1754), doubles (364) and sacrifice flies (73.) He also won four Gold Gloves. Can you name him?

Question #181

Name the pitcher who has the most career wins as a Chicago Cub?

Question #182

What Cub pitcher has the most wins in a single season in team history?

Question #183

Who managed the Cubs to their only two World Series championships?

Question #184

Who managed the Cubs to their last World Series appearance?

Question #185

Who had the lowest ERA in a single season for the Cubs?

Question #186

This four time Cub All Star outfielder drove in 110 runs during the season of the team's last trip to World Series. Can you name him?

Question #187

What one-time Cub pitcher gave up Ernie Banks' 400th career home run?

Question #188

What pitcher gave up Ernie Banks' final home run as a Cub in 1971?

Question #189

Name the one-time Cub pitcher who gave up Billy Williams' final home run as a Chicago Cub?

Question #190

Name the Hall Of Fame pitcher who gave up Ron Santo's 300th career home run?

Question #191

The Cubs received this future Hall Of Fame infielder in a trade with the Philadelphia Phillies for shortstop Ivan DeJesus. Can you name him?

Question #192

Name the Cub Hall Of Fame catcher who hit the famous home run in the "gloamin'" at Wrigley Field during the 1938 season?

Question #193

Name the pitcher who has the most strikeouts as a Chicago Cub?

Question #194

Name the Cub pitcher with the most home runs in a single season (post 1900)?

Question #195

Name the two players who are tied for the highest career batting average in Cub history?

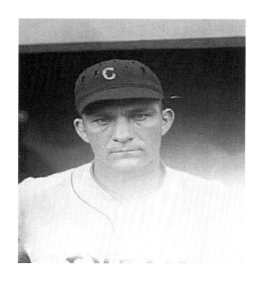

Question #196

What player has the most career home runs as a Chicago Cub?

Question #197

What player has the most career hits as a Chicago Cub (post 1900)?

Question #198

What player has the most career RBI's as a Chicago Cub (post 1900)?

Question #199

What pitcher has the most career saves in Chicago Cubs history?

Question #200

Name the player with the most hits in a single season by a Chicago Cub?

1908 World Champion Chicago Cubs

So You Call Yourself A Chicago Cubs Fan?

So You Call Yourself A Chicago Cubs Fan?

Quiz Answers

1. Whitey Lockman
2. Roe Skidmore
3. Jim Colborn
4. Andre Thornton
5. Mitch Williams
6. Bobby Bonds
7. Billy Williams
8. Willie Hernadez
9. Ralph Kiner
10. Phil Reagan
11. Jim Qualls
12. Bobby Hill
13. Ty Griffin
14. Fergie Jenkins
15. Jim Hickman
16. Sammy Sosa
17. Bill Hands
18. Kerry Wood
19. Greg Maddux
20. San Francisco Giants
21. Billy Williams
22. Gene Michael
23. Gene Baker
24. Ernie Banks
25. Brock Davis
26. Pete Lacock
27. Jerome Walton

28. Sam Jones
29. Ken Hubbs
30. Bill Veeck
31. Bill Stoneman
32. The Rifleman
33. Dennis Eckersley
34. Dennis Eckersley
35. Bobby Murcer
36. Billy Herman
37. Lee Smith
38. Frankie Frisch
39. Joe McCarthy
40. Leo Durocher
41. Milt Pappas
42. Miller Park in Milwaukee, WI
43. Don Cardwell
44. Harvey Kuenn
45. Ken Holtzman
46. Ken Holtzman
47. Ernie Banks
48. Hack Wilson
49. Andre Dawson
50. Don Kessinger
51. Lou Brock
52. Dave Smith
53. Willie Banks
54. Eddie Zambrano
55. Joe Niekro
56. Joe Carter
57. George Bell aka Jorge Bell
58. San Francisco Giants

59. Pat Jarvis
60. Rick Sutcliffe
61. Atlanta Braves
62. Josh Hamilton
63. Jason Seahorn
64. Shawon Dunston
65. Joe Carter
66. Brooks Kieschnick
67. Steve Trachsel
68. Moises Alou
69. Four
70. Joe Girardi
71. Jim Frey
72. Derrick May
73. Brant Brown
74. Ben Christensen
75. Greg Maddux
76. Hee-Seop Choi
77. Corey Patterson
78. Billy Hatcher
79. West Side Grounds
80. Weeghman Park
81. Cubs Park
82. None
83. West Side Grounds
84. 1926
85. 1929
86. West Side Grounds
87. Los Angeles, CA
88. Los Angeles Angels
89. Milt Pappas

90. Glenn Beckert
91. Randy Hundley
92. White Stockings
93. J.C. Martin
94. Calvin Schiraldi
95. Claude Passeau
96. Lou Boudreau
97. Jody Davis
98. Don Young
99. Chicago Orphans
100. Leo Durocher
101. Jorge Soler
102. Frank Chance
103. Seattle Mariners
104. Bill Madlock
105. Billy Williams
106. Bill North
107. Carmen Fanzone
108. Donnie Moore
109. Dave Kingman
110. Billy Williams
111. Gary Mathews
112. Derek Lee
113. Luis Montenez
114. Kris Bryant ($6.7 million)
115. Jorge Soler
116. Ryan Harvey
117. Shawon Dunston
118. Rafael Palmiero
119. Drew Hall
120. Don Schulze

121. Terry Hughes
122. Jon Garland
123. Dizzy Dean
124. Hippo Vaughn
125. Rick Reuschel
126. Phil Cavarretta
127. Mike Morgan
128. Rick Aguilera
129. Rogers Hornsby
130. Detroit Tigers (Four)
131. Kiki Cuyler
132. Charlie Root
133. Lon Warneke
134. Burleigh Grimes
135. Fred Merkle
136. Rick Monday
137. Chicago Colts
138. Detroit Tigers
139. Rick Reuschel
140. Ron Santo (traded for Steve Stone)
141. Steve Trout
142. Lee Elia
143. Preston Gomez
144. Rick & Paul Reuschel
145. Mike Tyson
146. Mordecai "Three Finger" Brown
147. Philadelphia Phillies
148. New York Mets
149. Alvin Dark
150. Bobby Thomson
151. The College Of Coaches

152. Charles Weeghman
153. Charles Murphy
154. Scott Sullivan (Cincinnati Reds in 2003)
155. Eric Plunk (Milwaukee Brewers)
156. Jose Lima (Houston Astros)
157. Joe Carter
158. Four
159. Jim Frey (1984)
160. Jim Tracy
161. Tony LaRussa
162. Grover Cleveland Alexander (1920)
163. Grover Cleveland Alexander
164. Hippo Vaughn (1918)
165. Nomar Garciaparra
166. Frank Schulte (1911)
167. Chuck Klein
168. Gabby Hartnett (1935)
169. Hank Sauer
170. Fergie Jenkins (1971)
171. Bruce Sutter (1979)
172. Randy Myers (53 in 1993)
173. Don Baylor
174. Kerry Wood (1998)
175. Jim Lefebvre
176. Don Baylor
177. Geovany Soto (2008)
178. Dontrelle Willis
179. Bill Madlock (1979 co-winner with Jon Matlack New York Mets)
180. Mark Grace

181. Charlie Root (201)
182. Mordecai "Three Finger" Brown (209 wins in 1908)
183. Frank Chance (1907 & 1908)
184. Charlie Grimm (1945)
185. Mordecai "Three Finger" Brown (1.04 in 1906)
186. Andy Pafko
187. Curt Simmons (of St. Louis Cardinals 9-2-65 at Wrigley Field)
188. Jim McGlothlin (of Cincinnati Reds 8-24-71 at Wrigley Field #513)
189. Lynn McGlothen (of St. Louis Cardinals 9-28-74 at Wrigley Field)
190. Tom Seaver (of New York Mets 9-21-71)
191. Ryne Sandberg
192. Gabby Hartnett
193. Fergie Jenkins (2038)
194. Fergie Jenkins (274 in 1970)
195. Riggs Stephenson & Bill Madlock (.336)
196. Sammy Sosa (545)
197. Ernie Banks (2583)
198. Ernie Banks (1636)
199. Lee Smith (180)
200. Rogers Hornsby (229 in 1929)

About The Author:

David Furgess was born in Bridgeport, Connecticut on February 27, 1961. He has been a die hard Chicago Cubs fan since 1968. He currently lives in Salem, CT. He is also author of *Chicago Cubs Minor League Report 2013* and *Chicago Cubs Fact Book 2013*. He is currently working on the *Chicago Cubs Almanac 2014* (which is due in spring 2014.) For details on all books by David Furgess please visit shibeparkpublishing@blogspot.com

David Furgess